WHY Would a ★ DOG ★ NEED A PARACHUTE?

Jo Foster studied history at the University of Cambridge and then worked for several years on TV history documentaries as a researcher and assistant producer. She is the author of the History Spies series. Jo lives in Winchester with her family.

JO FOSTER

WHY Would a DOG NEED A PARACHUTE?

ILLUSTRATED BY
ANDREW WIGHTMAN

IWM
IMPERIAL WAR MUSEUMS

In association with
Imperial War Museums

MACMILLAN CHILDREN'S BOOKS

First published 2014 by Macmillan Children's Books
a division of Macmillan Publishers Limited
20 New Wharf Road, London N1 9RR
Basingstoke and Oxford
Associated companies throughout the world
www.panmacmillan.com

In association with Imperial War Museums
IWM.org.uk

ISBN 978-1-4472-2618-5

1 3 5 7 9 8 6 4 2

A CIP catalogue record for this book is available from
the British Library.

Printed and bound by CPI Group (UK) Ltd, Croydon CR0 4YY

For Dan and Nat, with love

The Second World War 1939-1945

Why did the Second World War start?

Why was food rationed?

Could you still buy sweets?

Why were spies important?

To find out, turn the page!

1

How did the war start?

All over Britain, at just before 11:15 a.m. on a Sunday morning, people tuned in their radios to hear the Prime Minister say: 'This country is at war with Germany.' It was 3 September 1939, and the Second World War had begun.

But of course, the PM hadn't just woken up that morning and decided to start a war. That's not how these things work. The war wasn't a huge surprise; most of the people listening to their radios would have been expecting it. In the Prime Minister's speech, he also said how sad he was that there had to be a war, and how he had tried everything to avoid it. But Adolf Hitler, the leader of Germany, would do anything to get his way and the only way to stop him was to fight back.

Adolf Hitler had been making trouble for years. First Hitler increased the size of his army, and then he started to occupy other countries in Europe. In 1938 he marched his soldiers into Austria and announced that it was now part of Germany — and he didn't plan to stop there. Britain and France, the other two most powerful countries in Europe, saw that Hitler was getting greedy for other countries' land, but they weren't sure what to do about it.

Before TVs were commonplace, most people received their news from listening to the 'wireless' or radio.

3

Did Britain and France try to stop Hitler in other ways first?

Yes. They tried asking Hitler diplomatically to stop, even *agreeing* to let him occupy just *part* of the next country on his list, Czechoslovakia. After all, neither Britain nor France had much spare money for paying soldiers or buying guns, and as it was only twenty years since the end of the devastating First World War they were desperate to avoid another fight.

But asking nicely didn't work. Hitler broke his promise, and went ahead and invaded the whole of Czechoslovakia. Next on the list was Poland. Britain and France realized they had to get tough, and promised Poland that if Hitler invaded, they would send soldiers to help. This didn't stop Hitler either — the Germans attacked Poland on 1 September. Two days later, after warning Hitler again and giving him one last chance to back down, Britain and France declared war on Germany and the British Prime Minister, Neville Chamberlain, gave everyone the sad news over the radio.

But that's just the story of how it happened, not *why*. To really find out how Europe had got into this mess, we have to rewind a bit.

Some of the trouble came down to money. In the 1930s, there was a terrible economic crisis all over the world. In lots of countries in Europe, people lost their jobs and couldn't afford to buy food. Prices were getting higher and higher. Life was really hard, and the usual crowd of politicians didn't seem to be helping. So in some countries, the people turned to extreme kinds of politics, including Fascism and Communism.

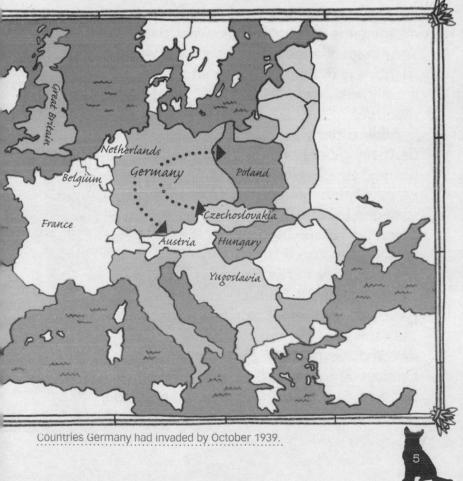

Countries Germany had invaded by October 1939.

How were Fascism and Communism different to Democracy?

In democracies such as France and Great Britain, the public could (and still can) vote for who they want to be in charge. During the 1930s, Fascist and Communist countries appointed strong leaders, who would not allow *any* other political parties or different ideas. They were known as 'dictators', meaning everyone had to do what they said. They made it appear as if their way was the only 'right' way of doing things, and the people were not allowed to publicly disagree.

Adolf Hitler was Germany's dictator. The German people were especially keen to find someone to solve their problems for one big reason: they had been on the losing side in the First World War, and it hadn't gone well for them. Like the other countries involved, Germany had lost a huge number of young men in the last war, and had spent more money than it could afford. But as the loser, Germany had also been

Adolf Hitler was Germany's dictator.

punished for its part in starting the war. It had to pay money to the winners to say sorry, and it had also had land which it thought should be part of Germany taken away and given to other countries. And, to make sure Germany didn't start another war, the winners had made it agree to keep its army and navy small.

All this felt like an insult to lots of Germans, including Hitler, who had fought in the First World War. As well as having bad money problems, Germany also felt humiliated by everything that had happened since the First World War.

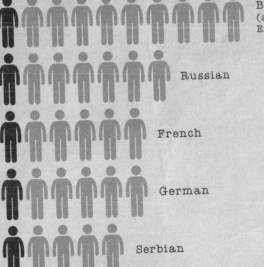

Deaths per number of men sent to fight in the First World War

British (and British Empire)

Russian

French

German

Serbian

How did Hitler persuade the German people that he should be in charge?

Hitler told the Germans what they wanted to hear: that they deserved to have more land and power, and that they deserved to regain their national pride. He made very passionate, impressive speeches which convinced people he knew what he was talking about. After being appointed Chancellor in 1939, he took charge and started on his plan to make Germany great — by grabbing land from the countries next door. So that's why Hitler invaded Poland in September 1939, and that's why Britain and France declared war on Germany, and that's how the Second World War began.

So what happened next?

This all brings us back to that Sunday morning, 3 September 1939. As soon as war was declared, new and frightening things started to happen. Loud, wailing air-raid sirens sounded over London, warning people that bombs might be dropped at any moment.

Huge silver balloons appeared in the sky over the nation's cities. Everyone was given a box with a gas mask in it. But where were all the soldiers, sailors and airmen rushing off to, and what would they be doing when they got there? Read on for all the answers!

Everyone in Britain was issued with a gas mask in case of a poison gas attack.

Who else was on our side?

In 1939, Britain had quite a team of friends and helpers. As well as England, Scotland and Wales, Britain had its 'Dominions' (Ireland, Canada, Australia, New Zealand and South Africa) and also the British Empire (including India, and many countries in Asia, Africa and the Caribbean). In all, about a quarter of all the people in the world were ruled over by Britain in some way.

Most countries in the Empire didn't get a choice about whether to join the war or not — if Britain was fighting, so were they. It was different for the Dominions, who could decide for themselves. Once Britain declared war, Australia, New Zealand, South Africa and Canada all decided to join in on her side, while Ireland stayed neutral — meaning it didn't join either side.

Britain, together with the Empire and Dominions, was part of a bigger group too, called the 'Allies' (meaning someone who's on your side). At the start of the war, the other main

Ally was France. There were also refugees from other countries which were attacked by Germany over the course of the war, like Poland, Greece and Belgium, who fought alongside Britain and France. The situation kept on changing: France got scrubbed out of the list of Allies in 1940, when the Germans invaded. And in 1941, two major powers joined the Allies: the Soviet Union (Russia) and America. The Russians thought they had agreed not to go to war against the Germans right up until Hitler invaded Russia; and the Americans were planning to stay out of the war, right up until Japan attacked Pearl Harbor, an important American base in Hawaii.

The Japanese attack on Pearl Harbor in 1941 brought the Americans into the war.

Who was the enemy?

The side fighting against the Allies was called the Axis. The word 'axis' means 'pivot', like the point in the middle which a wheel turns around — the idea was that the countries on the Axis side all turned around the same point to work together. Germany, Japan and Italy were the main Axis powers.

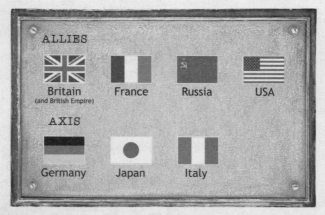

For people in Britain, the face of the enemy was that of Adolf Hitler, the leader of Germany and head of the Nazi Party. It was Hitler who had made the decision to invade Poland, causing Britain to declare war; it was Hitler who ordered his air force, the Luftwaffe, to bomb British cities; and it was Hitler whose army swept through France and then threatened to invade Britain.

Hitler was head of a political party known as the Nazis, who had promised to make Germany great and strong again. Once the German people voted the Nazis into power, they crushed anyone who disagreed with them. And there were very good reasons for disagreeing with the Nazis.

What did the Nazis believe?

The Nazis had some horrible ideas for how to make Germany strong. They planned to invade other countries to get more land for the Germans, and never mind the people who were living there already. They also planned to get rid of people they thought were weak or evil. The Nazis believed that everyone in the world could be divided into different races, and that some races were better than others. They thought that the Germans were the very best examples of the very best 'race' of people: the Aryans. The Aryans were supposed to be blond and blue-eyed — although if you look at a picture of Hitler you'll see he had dark hair.

The Nazis wanted to 'grow' their race, so German women were given a gold medal if they had eight children or more.

Why did Nazis think Aryans were the best?

The Nazis' ideas about the Aryans were wrong and dangerous — and sometimes ridiculous. Leading Nazi Heinrich Himmler was so keen to prove how wonderful the Aryans were that he set up an archaeological institute to investigate their history. They were supposed to dig up evidence of the glorious achievements of the ancestors of modern Germans. Researchers from the institute studied folk music and ancient art, and travelled the world coming up with strange theories about the history of the Aryans. Himmler also paid an archaeologist to find the Holy Grail, a mythical cup which was supposed to have been missing for hundreds of years.

The Holy Grail was believed to be a chalice or dish with mythical powers.

According to the Nazis, anyone who wasn't Aryan was worth *less* as a human being than an Aryan, so it was only right that they could be cleared out of the way to make room for the more important Germans. Of all the groups of people, or ethnicities, Nazis especially hated the

Jews. They blamed Jewish people for pretty much everything that had ever gone wrong, including Germany losing the First World War. After the Nazis came to power, things got steadily worse for German Jews; laws were brought in barring them from being legal citizens, owning businesses or from marrying non-Jewish Germans. By 1941, Jews also had to wear yellow 'badges of shame' in the shape of a Star of David on their clothes, to make them easier to spot, and were often victims of violence. In fact, as the war went on, the Nazis' hatred of the Jews led them to start a terrible process known now as the Holocaust.

A Polish Jew, forced to wear a Star of David in Warsaw.

What was the Holocaust?

A 'holocaust' is an old word for a sacrifice, and 'the Holocaust' is the name for the mass killing of around six million Jewish people by the Nazis and their collaborators. The Nazis decided they needed to get rid of the Jews permanently — first, they would go after all the Jews in Europe, and then once they won the war, they would wipe out all the Jews in the world. Nothing like this killing of a whole ethnicity of people had ever been attempted before. In Russia and Eastern Europe, Jewish people were gathered together and shot. In some European cities, the Nazis created 'ghettos', small blocked-off parts of the city which were the only places where Jews were allowed. From 1942 onwards, people in these ghettos were taken by train to labour camps or death camps. In labour camps, prisoners had to work long hours in terrible conditions until they died. In death camps, they were killed, often using poison gas pumped into closed rooms called gas chambers. The Holocaust was so dreadful that many museums and organizations such as the Imperial War Museum in London have devoted huge efforts to telling people about what happened here in Europe.

17

What sorts of people fought in the war?

All sorts. And there were all sorts of reasons why someone might sign up to join the army, navy or air force, as well. Some people simply wanted to stop Hitler — they thought that his ideas were wrong, or that he wouldn't stop until he'd taken over the whole of Europe. Some people wanted to protect Britain from invasion. Some just wanted a job and a wage. And others didn't really want to fight at all, but had to; 'conscription' in Britain started in 1939, which meant that men of fighting age were forced to go to war.

Allied fighters from all over the world came to Britain on their way to war in Europe. So people from India, the USA, Poland, Jamaica and many other countries suddenly turned up in Britain in 1939, where lots of people had never seen anyone who wasn't white before. Now people with different colour skin, different languages and different religions were all meeting up and serving together. For instance, ten thousand men and women from the Caribbean volunteered to serve Britain in the war, even though the British government wouldn't even let black people have the vote in the Caribbean. Just like in England, the Caribbean had blackouts, air-raid drills and rationing, so everyone had the restrictions and shortages of wartime, even if they stayed at home.

A British soldier, sailor and RAF airman.

What did recruits from the Empire do in the war?

Recruits from the Empire served in all branches of the services. At the beginning of the war, black people weren't allowed to join the Royal Air Force. After this rule changed in 1941, lots of West Indian men joined the RAF to serve Britain. One of those who joined up was a young man from Guyana named Cy Grant. He trained to be a navigator. Unluckily for Cy, his plane was set on fire while flying over Holland, and he had to jump out with a parachute. Even more unluckily, he was captured by the Germans and sent to a prison camp — the same camp that is shown in the film *The Great Escape*. Things looked up for Cy after the war, though, when he became famous for singing Caribbean calypso songs.

How old were the people who fought?

At first, men aged between 18 and 41 could be 'called up' for service in the British armed forces. Officially, you had to be 18 before you could go to war in the army or the RAF. Younger boys could join the Navy from the age of 14 for certain jobs. But the war offered excitement, travel and adventure for some boys, and plenty of teenagers lied about their ages to join up early. Adult life started earlier for wartime kids than it does now. In the 1940s, children only had to stay at school until they were 14, and in wartime many of them left even earlier than that. While some 13- and 14-year-olds were finishing school and starting jobs with the grown-ups, others went off to war.

BE AN AIRMAN

APPLY TO THE NEAREST R.A.F. RECRUITING DEPOT
OR WRITE TO THE INSPECTOR OF RECRUITING
VICTORY HOUSE, KINGSWAY, LONDON W.C.2.

Exciting-looking adverts such as this encouraged men and young boys to join the armed forces.

How old was the youngest Britain in uniform to die during the war?

In July 1941, a cabin boy named Reginald Earnshaw was killed on the merchant navy ship the SS *North Devon*. He had said he was 15 when he joined up, so that he would be able to go abroad and see some of the action, but this was a lie. He was actually only 14, making him the youngest Britain in uniform to die in World War Two.

Reginald Earnshaw joined the merchant navy aged only 14.

Many more young people had hair-raising experiences during the war. John Chinnery, for instance, had gone to sea as a young boy. He was aged 13 when his ship was hit by a torpedo (an underwater self-propelled weapon). Luckily for John, his crewmates grabbed him and chucked him into a lifeboat, saving his life. Less luckily, he hadn't had time to get dressed when this happened, so he arrived in Glasgow some time after being rescued wearing only his pants and a waterproof mac that someone had given him.

At the start of the war, the Allied armies were full of keen, healthy young recruits. As the years went by, the numbers of spare young men back home fell, and older men started to be called up. Things were the same in the German army. In the last years of the war, when the Germans were on the losing side and having to fight harder than ever, they were also running out of men of fighting age.

A British Royal Navy ship in harbour in Malta during the conflict.

So how did the Germans find more soldiers?

They began to send members of the Nazis' youth organization, the Hitler Youth, off to war at the age of 16 and even younger. When the Allied armies arrived in Germany, soldiers reported being shocked at meeting children of primary school age defending their country 'to the death'.

Members of the Hitler Youth.

In Britain, boys who were too young to join up, and men who were too old, could always join the Army Cadet Force or the Home Guard instead. The Home Guard was formed in order to defend the country if the Germans invaded. It was full of men who were unable to serve in the armed forces, often because of their age. If Britain ever had been invaded, the Home Guard could have had a key part in the fighting, as would Churchill's 'Secret Army', who had been trained to 'fight on' in the case of invasion.

Could women fight as well?

Not exactly, no. Women weren't allowed to fight in the British services, but just because they couldn't fight, it doesn't mean they couldn't help win the war. There were all sorts of jobs in the army, navy and air force which didn't involve fighting: women drove and repaired cars and trucks, flew aeroplanes, sent messages over the radio, decoded enemy messages, kept a lookout for enemy planes, and fired the huge anti-aircraft guns which protected British cities from bombers. In 1941, the government started conscripting women for jobs to support the war effort. They could choose whether they joined the armed forces or a civilian organization, either working in industry or on the land.

Posters recruiting women into the Women's Auxiliary Air Force.

Was it dangerous for women who worked to support the war effort?

Some women worked long days on farms as 'land girls' to keep the food supply going while male farm workers were at war; others drove ambulances through air raids and helped

Women's Land Army Training, Cannington, Somerset, England, 1940.

people with terrible injuries. Because the Second World War was a 'total war', fought in cities as well as on battlefields, a woman doing a dangerous job like this could see just as much action and devastation as her brother who went to war abroad.

In other countries, the rules were different, and women did fight in some armies. The Russian army had more women fighting than any other country. As well as firing anti-aircraft guns, Russian women flew fighter planes and even trained as sharp-shooting snipers.

Where did the fighting happen?

The Second World War really did happen all over the world. There was fighting in Europe, from Norway to Greece and from Russia to England; in North Africa, China, Japan, South-East Asia, and in the Atlantic and Pacific Oceans. Although Germany was the nearest enemy for Britain, the Axis weren't just trying to take over Europe; on the other side of the world, Japan was fighting to try to get extra land in China and elsewhere in Asia.

Each different war zone had new unpleasant challenges. In North Africa, soldiers fought in the desert. On top of the heat, thirst and flies, there were fierce sandstorms which stung their skin and obscured their vision so they could hardly see which way to go.

A soldier battling his way through a sandstorm in the Western Desert, North Africa.

27

In Eastern Europe, Finland and Russia, armies battled through snow, ice and painfully low temperatures. Other soldiers fought up mountains, in dense, humid jungles in Asia, and in the streets of cities like Stalingrad and Berlin. And that was just the fighting that happened on land!

Where else was the war fought if not on land?

The Second World War was also fought at sea and in the air. Sailors served on huge warships and underwater on cramped submarines. Aeroplanes flew over war zones

This British pilot is just about to start a night patrol, looking out for enemy planes.

to fire bullets and drop bombs on the enemy, and pilots also fought other pilots in fighter planes. And everyone fighting in the Second World War came home with very different war stories, depending on where they had been.

What was it like to fly a fighter plane?

In the Battle of Britain in the summer and autumn of 1940, fighter planes were vitally important. When Germany was planning to invade Britain, they knew they would have to get rid of Britain's Royal Air Force, or RAF, first or the invasion wouldn't

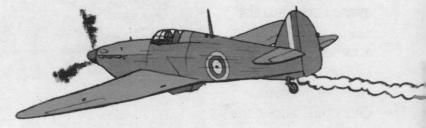

stand a chance. The RAF fought Germany's Luftwaffe (which is German for 'air weapon') in the sky over the south and east of England. The pilots who flew these planes became heroes to the British public; they were stopping the Germans from invading right over people's heads, and if you were in the right place in Sussex or Kent you could have a close-up view of their battles just by looking up.

The job of a fighter pilot was horribly dangerous, but on the plus side, it has been said that pilots never had to buy their own drinks in a pub — the uniform made them instant celebrities. There's a famous quote by the new Prime Minister, Winston Churchill, about the

This RAF Air Cadet was training to be a pilot.

pilots in the Battle of Britain: 'Never in the field of human conflict was so much owed by so many to so few.' Britain won the battle, and these plucky pilots had stopped Germany from invading.

What kinds of planes did British pilots fly?

The two most important types of British fighter planes were Hurricanes and Spitfires. Although you're more likely to

A Hurricane plane – ready to be 'scrambled'.

have heard of a Spitfire, the Hurricane shot down more than half of the German planes that were downed in the Battle of Britain.

Two Supermarine Spitfires in flight.

Both types of plane were only big enough for one person, but had eight machine guns which the pilot could operate. The pilot had to navigate, fly the plane, and fire the guns, all by himself. Because the guns were fixed in position, the whole plane had to be pointed at the target, rather than just aiming the guns.

What was it like inside the cockpit of a British fighter?

The author Roald Dahl flew Hurricanes during the war, and wrote about the experience in his book, *Going Solo*. 'You are in a small metal cockpit where just about everything is made of riveted aluminium. There is a plexiglass hood over your head and a sloping bullet-proof windscreen in front of you . . . you can turn your head and you can move your arms and legs, but the rest of your body is strapped so tightly into the tiny cockpit that you cannot move.'

The cramped space was uncomfortable, the noise was deafening, and the thin walls of the aeroplane also made flying high in the air a very cold experience. The silk scarves which pilots wore were partly to stop their jackets from chafing their necks, especially as they had to keep constantly turning their heads to look all around them for other planes; the scarves also helped to keep them warm in sub-zero temperatures.

However uncomfortable it was to fly a Spitfire or a Hurricane, coping with the extreme danger that the pilots faced was worse. It was reckoned that during the Battle of Britain, pilots who flew for a period of six months were bound to be shot down at some point. Fighting this air battle was exhausting and terrifying. Even the waiting was a terrible strain on pilots' nerves. They never knew when they would get the call that German planes had been spotted, and it was time to 'scramble', or hurry to the planes and get up in the air. And when they did get the call, they knew it was quite possible they would be shot down and injured or killed.

Where did soldiers go to the loo?

This thorny question is often asked by school groups visiting the Imperial War Museum. Of course, if they're on base or somewhere civilized, soldiers use the toilet like everyone else. But in the middle of a battle, you can't just stop what you're doing and head off to the loo. And there certainly aren't any toilets in a tank.

So . . . where did soldiers go to the loo in a tank or during battle?

Well, if you could find some sort of container, you could always go in there, but the unpleasant answer is that if that wasn't possible you might have to simply go in your uniform. But let's not forget, there were many far worse things about being in a battle.

What did the different sides wear?

Lots of different things! So many different sorts of people fought in the Second World War, as different ranks of sailors, soldiers and airmen, that they needed lots of different uniforms for all their jobs. It's not as simple as sports teams all choosing a colour top to wear so that you can tell which side is which. Every country's navy wore blue or white, but there were plenty of differences to spot between the shapes and colours of all the uniforms.

What each fighter wore varied according to things like where they were fighting (it's no good wearing shorts when you're off to war in Russia in January), what sort of kit they needed to have with them, and what the armed forces were used to wearing. So, some Italian army uniforms included a feathery hat, and French sailors' hats had pompoms on top — not because they were useful, but because that's what they had always worn.

Second World War uniforms

Second World War uniforms varied widely. For example, Japanese army officers had beige uniforms for fighting in tropical climates, white helmets (good for hot weather) and carried a samurai sword!

A samurai sword was a deadly close-range weapon.

German soldiers wore field grey (which was actually a kind of greyish green colour), with a distinctively shaped helmet.

Soviet soldiers were dressed for fighting in the Russian winter. Their jackets were stuffed with insulating material to keep them warm.

What did British soldiers wear?

The basic uniform for British soldiers was:

- A short jacket known as a battledress blouse — the British army had to supply hundreds of thousands of sets of uniform. By cutting the jackets shorter, they could save on cloth, which was in short supply.

- A pair of trousers with pockets — one for holding a map, and one for a basic first aid kit.
- A field service cap or, from late 1944, a wool beret, with the badge of the soldier's regiment on the front.
- A steel helmet, vital for protecting the head from bullets and flying shrapnel when in battle.
- Tough hobnail boots.
- Combat webbing: a belt with shoulder straps, which came with attachments so that a soldier could carry all the kit he needed. This might include a bottle of water, plenty of bullets, a bayonet (a sharp knife which fitted on to the end of a rifle for fighting someone close to you), an entrenching tool (a folding spade for digging trenches) and a rucksack for spare clothes, food and cooking utensils.

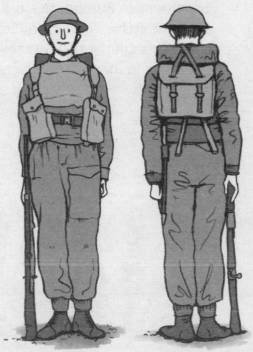

What were the British uniforms made of?

Both the jacket and trousers were made of coarse wool, which was good for wearing in cold, damp conditions in Europe, but it had a downside: it could be itchy. To save soldiers' necks from nasty chafing, artificial silk was sewn into the jacket collars, and more padding could be added by wearing a white bandage as a neck covering.

These British soldiers are wearing their woollen uniforms for fighting in Europe.

Wool uniforms were no good for men fighting in the desert heat of summer in North Africa. Instead, they had cotton summer uniforms, and could wear shorts instead of trousers. But the combat webbing, with all its heavy attachments, had to be worn in spite of the heat.

This British soldier is wearing a cotton uniform with shorts – much more suitable for the desert!

Uniforms for use in the desert were also a lighter colour than the brown wool worn in Europe, to help soldiers blend in with the desert. To really help them hide in their surroundings, armies developed proper camouflage patterns as the war went on. Fighting in the jungle required a different camouflage from fighting in a French city. At first, Allied soldiers noticed that some German troops were wearing uniforms covered in brown and green dots, which worked to help keep them hidden. But when some Allied snipers tried wearing this same pattern, they hit a problem: when their own comrades did manage to spot them, they mistook them for Germans and fired on them!

What about other services? Did they all have the same uniforms?

No, other services had different uniforms from the Army. Sailors in the Royal Navy wore . . . navy blue, of course. The other distinctive parts of a sailor's uniform included a particular cut of wide-leg 'bell-bottomed' trousers, a cap without a peak, and a collar with a point at the front and a square shape at the back. In the Royal Air Force, uniforms were a greyish blue version of army uniforms but also included a shirt, collar and tie.

How often did soldiers get to go home?

For people in the armed forces, time off is called 'leave' (because you have 'leave', or permission, to go where you want). During World War Two, soldiers had regular leave, but would only get to go home if it was possible to travel back. For men fighting in Asia or Africa, this journey would have taken far too long. They would still get leave, but would have to have spent it near where they were posted, which meant exotic holidays in India or Egypt for some soldiers who might never have left Britain before the war. Because travel was difficult, some soldiers who were posted a long way from Britain never went home for the entire six-year war.

41

What was 'compassionate leave'?

On top of regular leave, there was extra time off which a soldier could get if he had family problems, called 'compassionate leave'. Lots of men who had been away for a long time eventually got letters to say that their wives were getting fed up with being at home on their own, and they were sometimes given compassionate leave to go home and try to patch things up. This didn't always help: after the war, when the men returned home to their families, many of them found it was just too difficult to live together again, and the divorce rate shot up to twice what it had been before the war.

Dear Peter,

Things have been difficult with you being gone for so long and I am starting to feel like I don't know you any more. I am worried that we are becoming strangers.

When can you come home? If it is not soon I do not know what I will do. The children all miss you very much. Please write soon,

Mary

What happened to people who were caught by the enemy?

It depended which side they were fighting on, and who had caught them. A soldier fighting in Asia who was taken prisoner by the Japanese army was unlucky; Japanese camps for prisoners of war (known as POWs) were very unpleasant. At the time, most Japanese soldiers believed that a soldier should keep on fighting and never give up, so anyone who was taken prisoner by the enemy must be cowardly and not worth treating well. Prisoners in Japanese camps were often starved and given very little medical treatment when they got ill. They were also forced to work, often so hard that they died, and severe punishments were given for anyone who disobeyed orders or tried to escape. Overall, about a quarter of all soldiers from Great Britain who were captured by the Japanese died while in captivity.

What about POW camps in Germany?

Russian soldiers who were captured by the Germans were also very badly treated. According to Nazi beliefs, the Russians were inferior people, who didn't deserve to be dealt with in a civilized way. Their camps had overcrowding and terrible conditions, and prisoners were given very little food. Many of them were worked to death or simply killed. Over three *million* Russians died in these camps.

If a British or American soldier was captured by the Germans, he would have been a bit luckier: he would probably have been reasonably well looked after, though there wasn't much food, and many POWs were made to work very hard. Prisoners could also sometimes send letters home and receive Red Cross food parcels, although any letters coming in or going out would have been opened and censored. Some POWs even managed to get an education while in the camps, by

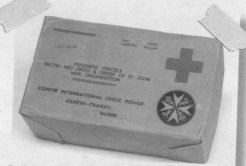

Red cross parcels had food rations in them as well as toiletries such as soap.

doing correspondence courses by letter.

In a camp with fairly good conditions, boredom was often a terrible problem for officers — who were not usually forced to work like other POWs. To pass the time, prisoners turned to all sorts of hobbies. Some knitted amazing jumpers and blankets with home-made needles and yarn taken from old clothes. In one German camp, a group of British prisoners formed an amateur bird-watching society. They spent days on end, from dawn to dusk, carefully observing the birds outside the wire of the camp and noting what they saw. Eventually, they made important new scientific discoveries about the species they saw.

What was the Geneva Convention?

Before the war, most countries had agreed to stick to an agreement called the Geneva Convention, which included rules on how prisoners should be looked after in wartime. At the end of the war, new rules were added to try to avoid some of the awful things that had happened to prisoners in the wartime camps.

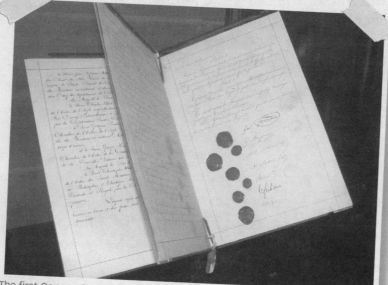

The first Geneva Convention was created in 1864 – this is the original document.

How did commanders tell everyone what to do?

For any commander sending soldiers to fight in a war, it's vitally important to be able to communicate with them. The commanders have to be able to send orders to their troops, and the armies around the world have to be able to send back information on how the battle's gone, where they think the enemy is, and how many more bullets or tins of baked beans they need. They didn't have the Internet or mobile phones, but the armies of the Second World War did have some pretty ingenious technology for getting messages across.

How did people communicate without the Internet or mobiles?

They could send a letter through the post. But letters at home were even slower than usual because so many men had gone off to join the army that the Post Office was struggling on without most of its usual staff. It had to cut its deliveries and collections in half, slowing down the mail to a crawl. And as anyone knows who's ever waited for something important to come through the post, you can't run a decent war just using letters.

47

How else did people send messages?

Telephones had been invented a long time before the war. Telephones are definitely quicker when they're working, but they need lines — which there weren't many of out in the jungle

or at sea. Telephone wires also get cut easily when a bomb goes off. This was a problem at home, when cities like London were bombed, as well as abroad where the troops were fighting.

Instead of making a phone call or writing a letter, in the first half of the twentieth century you could send a telegram. The message would be sent electronically, and delivered by the postman faster than a letter could arrive. But you might not have been excited to get a telegram; they often brought bad news. Telegrams were used to

Telegrams usually came in yellow envelopes and often contained bad news.

tell a serviceman's family when he was wounded or killed, so people dreaded getting telegrams in wartime. And just like with a phone call, you need to be connected with wires to send a telegram.

Was there any way of sending a message without wires?

Luckily, yes there was. You might have heard people talking in old films about 'the wireless', meaning the radio. It's the same sort of technology as we still use to listen to shows on the radio today, except none of it was digital in the 1940s. To find out the war news, people back home relied on newspapers, radio reports, and 'newsreels' at the cinema.

What about TV? Had that been invented yet?

TV *had* been invented by the start of the Second World War, but hardly anyone had their own telly, and in Britain the TV signal was turned off all through the war. And it was going to be over *50 years* before people started getting their news from the Internet.

In battle, radios were vitally important. Not because soldiers were all desperate to hear the news or the latest hit songs, but because they had two-way radios like walkie-talkies which they could use to talk to their commanders. These old-fashioned radios were much bigger than walkie-talkies, and heavy to carry around.

In fact there were problems with all these methods of communication — technology is brilliant when it works, but not so good when it gets wet, or the wire's cut, or there's no signal. Often, the best way to get a message across was with the help of animals.

Animals? I'm pretty sure they didn't have talking animals back then. How could animals pass on messages?

You might be surprised. There are stories of the Germans setting up a special training school during the war, where they taught dogs to talk. Most of them didn't pass their exams well enough to hold a decent conversation, though!

Instead, real-life animal messengers would *literally* carry a message. A dog could be fitted with a special holder on its collar, in which soldiers could put rolled-up messages. Dogs were often much better at this job than people.

Infantry of the Queen's Regiment on the march with messenger dogs near Barham in Kent, 1941.

How were dogs better messengers than people?

American troops fighting in the jungle in New Guinea found that a dog could carry a message through the thick forest much quicker than a human soldier could — and they were also far quieter and less noticeable than a large soldier crashing around in the undergrowth. But the real message-carrying heroes of the war weren't talking dogs, but humble pigeons. Homing pigeons are used for racing because of their astounding sense of direction. In wartime, they were trained to think of their 'base' as home, so that soldiers could get messages home from wherever they were when other lines of communication were cut off. In February 1942, an RAF aeroplane crashed in the North Sea, leaving the survivors in a very sticky situation if they weren't rescued quickly. Their radio equipment had gone down with the plane, but luckily they had a pigeon with them.

This Canadian wireless operator is carrying two homing pigeons in boxes.

The anonymous pigeon, without even a message attached to her leg, flew straight back to base despite being covered in oil from the wreck — and her human colleagues worked out roughly where the plane would have been and sent out a search party. The pigeon saved the lives of her crew, and was honoured with a new name, Winkie, and also with her very own medal: the Dickin Medal for animal war heroes.

Why would a dog need a parachute?

Winkie the pigeon was the first animal to be given the Dickin Medal. Since her, over 60 animals have been honoured in the same way. They included cats, birds, horses and plenty of dogs, doing amazing jobs and saving lives.

Rifleman Khan was an Alsatian dog who worked with the

The Dickin Medal.

infantry in Europe. When he and his handler were on a small boat that was blown up off Holland in November 1944, they both plunged into the sea in freezing temperatures. Rifleman Khan swam to shore but then realized his friend was in trouble. So he saved the day by pulling his handler ashore, with his jacket

Rifleman Khan with his handler.

between Khan's teeth, as the enemy fired on them. The bond between Khan and his human handler was so strong that the handler was allowed to keep him after the war.

Not all heroic war dogs were big, tough Alsatians. Tipperary Beauty was a small wire-haired terrier who began her wartime career by finding a cat trapped under a table after an air raid. She continued to search for animal survivors of the bombing throughout the Blitz, and saved 62 more animals.

Perhaps one of the most daring war dogs was Rob, the Special Air Service paradog. With great bravery (and a specially designed harness), Rob is claimed to have made up to 20 parachute jumps over the course of the war and led his comrades on missions behind enemy lines.

Did any other animals use parachutes too?

One spectacular story of courageous spy pigeons happened after 1940, when most of north-west Europe was occupied by the Nazis. The British got together a staggering 16,544 pigeons, and put them each into a box with enough food for ten days — then attached the boxes to parachutes, flew over Europe, and dropped them. The plan was that some of the pigeons would be found by civilians who wanted to help beat the Nazis, who would write down useful information about where the German army positions were, tie it to the pigeon's leg, and then release the pigeon to take the note back home. Only 1,842 plucky birds returned — one of them carrying a very long and helpful note together with hand-drawn maps showing exactly where the Germans were.

What else did animals do? You're not going to tell me they fought in the war too?

Sometimes animals did get involved in the fighting. The Americans briefly got quite excited about the idea of using bats to attack cities in Japan — and it wasn't going to be much fun for the bats. The idea was to attach a tiny firebomb to each bat, and drop it from a plane with a parachute. The bats would then crawl into spaces inside buildings where they like to roost, then chew off their parachutes — triggering the bombs which would start a fire. Luckily for countless innocent bats, preliminary tests by the US Army found this to be a stupid idea.

How else did animals serve their countries?

There were plenty of better ways for animals to serve their humans in the war. Dogs famously have an amazing sense of smell, which means they were great for doing guard duty as they could smell out any strangers in the area. Many dogs also worked in British cities after air raids (see page 71), finding injured people and dead bodies which had been buried by rubble. And dogs' noses made them useful for one especially dangerous job: sniffing out land mines underground, to warn soldiers crossing minefields and to help show bomb disposal squads where they needed to make a bomb safe.

Animals could also help with a vitally important job in a world war: shifting the huge amounts of weapons, food, communications equipment and so on that the soldiers needed to wherever the fighting was. Even though in the Second World War

there were cars, trucks and planes, animals were often the best means of transport across remote country where petrol was short. In North Africa, camels could be the best way to carry equipment around. Elsewhere, the British and American armies used mules, a cross between a horse and a donkey. Mules could

Circus elephants clear bomb damage in Hamburg, 1945.

carry heavy loads across rough ground where a truck might have got stuck. The same was true of elephants, who worked for the British Army in Burma, but the elephants also had an extra talent. Having worked for timber companies in the teak forests, Burmese elephants were fantastic at carefully picking up and moving huge tree trunks — which made them expert bridge-builders when the army needed to cross a river.

While a horse might be a handy animal to have in Britain, or an elephant in the jungle, armies in the Second World War found themselves in all kinds of places and weather. For armies in the African desert, camels were the most useful animal to have around. And when the British started sending weapons and supplies to their

Ethiopian camel troops transporting supplies in Abyssinia (now Ethiopia), 1941.

Russian allies, they sent ships on a dangerous and chilly journey across the Arctic Sea. Once all this

stuff arrived in port in frozen northern Russia, it had to go overland to wherever it was needed — so herds of reindeer were roped in to help. And you thought they were just for Christmas.

Who had the best weapons?

In theory, Germany did. The Germans spent a lot of money and effort on developing fantastic technology. Their tanks, called Panzers, were cutting-edge: each had a powerful cannon at the front, two machine guns, and were lightweight

A German Panzer tank.

with multiple wheels to help them move easily.
German aeroplanes were roughly as good as Allied
planes, and so were their guns.

But that's not the whole story. A good gun
isn't just one that can shoot further and more
accurately than the rest. For instance, the German
Mauser rifle and the British Lee Enfield .303 rifle
were about as useful as each other for shooting a
target a long way away. But when someone fired
a Mauser, there was a big flash of light at the end
as the bullet came out — which was a problem if
you were trying to hide from the people you were
shooting. A flash of light could be like a big red
arrow showing the enemy where to aim to get rid
of you.

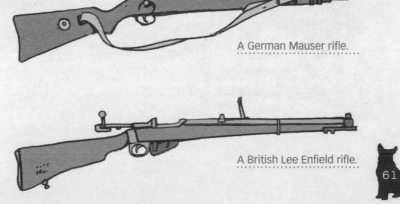

A German Mauser rifle.

A British Lee Enfield rifle.

What other sorts of new weapons were invented?

The Germans developed terrifying flying bombs, called V-1s or 'doodlebugs', which could reach all the way to London from across the Channel. Since the start of the war, the

A V-1 or 'doodlebug'.

British had been flying huge silver balloons, known as 'barrage balloons', on the way in to each city. Barrage balloons were filled with hydrogen to make them float, and tied to the ground with strong steel cables which could cut the wings off passing aeroplanes. The aim of the balloons was to make the German planes fly higher than they would

A barrage balloon being deployed in Kent.

like to, therefore making their bombing aim worse. But that wasn't all the German inventors had in store. Next they developed a frightening new rocket called the V-2 which flew higher and faster than any other missile. V-2s were the first thing made by humans which flew as high as space (62 miles above sea level).

The biggest problem with the flashy German technology was that it was expensive. The V-2 rocket was much faster and more powerful than the old V-1, but it also cost a staggering eighty times as much money. As the war went on, the Germans needed masses of guns, tanks, planes, bombs and bullets, and they didn't have enough money or enough factories to produce them all. They had spent so much on developing new weapons, they couldn't afford enough of the old boring ones. And as if that wasn't bad enough, at the same time the Allies were bombing the areas where the German factories were making new weapons and ammunition.

What was the 'Big Week' campaign?

In February 1944, the Allies had a campaign known as 'Big Week' — for six days, the British and Americans sent over thousands of aeroplanes to bomb the German weapon factories and weaken Germany's fighting power.

Of course, it's no use having lots of fearsome weapons if your soldiers don't know how to fire a gun. Training for troops was just as important as developing weapons, and when it came to training their elite parachute regiments, the Allies had the edge.

Overall, although the Germans had some of the best weapons, it didn't do them much good as they couldn't produce enough of them.

What was the deadliest weapon of all?

During the Second World War, a whole new type of bomb was invented, which would change the world. It was the most powerful and terrible weapon there had ever been: the atomic bomb.

The idea for the atomic bomb came out of scientific research on atoms, tiny particles which make up everything you see around you, and which were the smallest bit of matter you could get — until scientists learned how to break them. European researchers discovered that you could split an atom by firing an even smaller particle, called a neutron, at it. Splitting an atom releases:

(a) more neutrons, and
(b) ENERGY.

Which meant that if someone could work out how, they could use these newly released neutrons to split some more atoms, and so on and so on, into a chain reaction. This chain reaction would be very fast indeed, and would release loads of energy, *very suddenly*, in the form of an explosion bigger than anything that had ever been seen before.

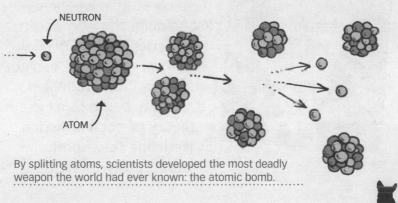

NEUTRON

ATOM

By splitting atoms, scientists developed the most deadly weapon the world had ever known: the atomic bomb.

Which country invented the atomic bomb first?

In 1939, Albert Einstein had just moved to America from Europe. He was Jewish and had left Europe to escape the Nazis. Together with two colleagues in the same position, he wrote a letter to the US President, Franklin D. Roosevelt, letting him know that scientists in Germany were trying to make this atomic bomb. Einstein and his friends wanted the Allies to build the bomb before the Nazis did.

Albert Einstein.

Franklin D. Roosevelt.

With help from Britain, Roosevelt set up the 'Manhattan Project' to develop atomic weapons. All through the war, an international team of scientists worked in secret to find out how to make a working bomb using the theory of nuclear fission (splitting the atom), desperately trying to do so before the Germans. In July 1945, the first atomic bomb was tested successfully, deep in the desert in New Mexico. It had taken so long that by the time the Manhattan Project team solved the puzzle, Germany was already out of the war.

The other enemy, though, was still fighting: Japan. The Allies knew they could beat Japan, but also that it could still take a very long time and cost the lives of lots more Allied servicemen. Now that the new US President, Harry S. Truman, had the atomic bomb, he had to decide whether to use it on Japan. He wanted to end the war quickly. He also knew that once the Americans had shown what the atomic bomb could do, other countries would think twice before messing with them in future.

Harry S. Truman.

What was 'Little Boy'?

The atomic bomb known as 'Little Boy'.

On 6 August 1945, an American plane dropped a bomb with the nickname 'Little Boy' on the Japanese city of Hiroshima. The explosion was so enormous that everything at the site disappeared instantly with the intense heat. Up to around a mile away from the blast, all wooden buildings were flattened. 70,000 people were killed straight away. Many more were injured. Some had horrible burns. Others, who had been further away when the bomb dropped, seemed fine at first but developed strange symptoms of 'radiation sickness' days later. By the end of the year, up to 70,000 more people died of their injuries.

Three days after the bombing of Hiroshima, another bomb was dropped. This one was nicknamed 'Fat Man', and was headed for the city of Kokura, but heavy cloud meant the bomber plane had to change course and saved the people of Kokura. Instead, the bomb was dropped on Nagasaki on 9 August, killing tens of thousands more people.

The big question about the dropping of the atomic bombs is usually this: **Was it the right thing to do?** The attacks on Hiroshima and Nagasaki definitely shortened the war, and saved the lives of many Allied and Japanese soldiers (and civilians) who would otherwise have died. But the bombs killed huge numbers of Japanese civilians in awful ways.

Those two huge explosions also changed the world dramatically. As soon as everyone had seen how terrible the atomic bomb was, the urgent new question became: How to cope? How could countries ever go to war again without destroying the whole world?

What was the Home Front?

When you hear about a war having different 'fronts', it means the places where the war is being fought. So you might read about soldiers 'going to the Front' or to 'the front line': if you imagine rows of soldiers lined up and marching into battle, it makes sense that the lines at the front are closest to the enemy, and the men in the back are safer.

In that case, how can there be such a thing as a Home Front? It means that what happens at home, or in Britain, is just as important as what happens on the army's front lines. In the two world wars that happened in the twentieth century, ordinary people at home were involved in the war whether they wanted to be or not — life changed for everyone, and by doing things like not wasting food, volunteering or not passing on gossip, everyone could help the war effort.

The Local Defence Volunteers turned into the Home Guard in 1940 and became better trained and equipped as the war went on.

What was the Blitz?

The 'Blitz' was the time
between 1940 and 1941
when the German air force
bombed Britain — not just every
now and then, but for months
on end.

The word 'Blitz' comes from
the German word 'Blitzkrieg',
meaning 'lightning war'. When
the Germans invaded other
countries in Europe at the start
of the war, they invented a
whole new way to do it. Using
motorbikes and tanks, the
German army moved faster
than had ever been seen in a war, swooping in at
lightning speed before anyone else had a chance to
fight back. This was the original 'lightning war'.

How did the Blitz begin?

For Britain, the Blitz meant something very different. Even in the 1930s, before the Second World War started, people had been worried that cities would be bombed by aeroplanes in the next war. As soon as the war began in September 1939, the government got everyone ready for the bombing by using air-raid sirens and shelters, and sending children out of the cities to safe places as evacuees (more on page 101). Barrage balloons appeared in

the skies to stop planes from flying too low over cities. Everyone was given a gas mask to carry all the time in case a plane dropped poison gas, though fortunately this didn't actually happen. For the first year of the war, the feared bombers didn't appear at all.

In the end, the Blitz on Britain's cities started almost by accident. In the late summer of 1940, German planes were bombing Britain's ports and other important places for the war effort — but

Firefighters during the Blitz on London's East End.

they were ordered not to hit towns where people lived. One night, two German planes were flying over England on a mission to bomb an oil refinery. Instead, they dropped their bombs on the city of London by mistake. The Prime Minister was furious, and decided to take revenge. The next night, he sent 81 RAF bombers to attack the German capital, Berlin. This, of course, made Hitler furious, and he threatened to flatten Britain's cities in return. On 7 September 1940, the first deliberate bombing raid of the Blitz turned East London into a firestorm. Suddenly, ordinary people trying to live their lives at home in the cities were under attack.

in a raid —

Open your door to passers-by — They need shelter too

The Trouble with Bombs

Although bombs had been dropped on towns and cities from zeppelins, Gotha and Giant bombers during the First World War, rapid changes in technology meant that by the 1940s aeroplanes could carry and deploy far greater volumes of bombs than ever before.

Both the British RAF and the German Luftwaffe were proud of their bomber aircraft, and boasted about how accurately they could pinpoint the exact target they wanted to hit.

A German bomber over London.

The truth was very different. Whichever side was dropping bombs, it was simply impossible to be certain of where they would fall.

In bad weather, it was hard for a pilot to see his target, and the wind could send bombs way off course. Because of this, trying to hit small targets was a waste of effort and of bombs. Only very big targets, like whole areas of cities, were easy enough to hit.

What was it like to live through the Blitz?

As you might imagine, it was an awful experience to see your home town bombed. Cities were dangerous places to be during the Blitz. In London, one in six people became homeless during the Blitz when bombs damaged or destroyed their houses.

Everyday life with the Blitz repair teams, London, 1944.

It wasn't just the danger of a bomb falling on you that made the Blitz feel different; everyday life changed in all sorts of ways. Just getting around at night became a struggle. This was because of the 'black-out' — city lights made it easy for German bombers to spot their targets, so all through the war streetlamps were turned off, car headlights had to be mostly covered up, and windows had to be covered

I've got 9 lives YOU haven't

LOOK OUT IN THE

BLACKOUT

There's danger on the roads

Vehicles driving with no lights made the roads much more dangerous at night.

with thick black curtains to stop any light getting out of buildings after dark. The streets were so gloomy that in the first few months of the war, nearly twice as many people were injured in traffic accidents as before.

There were also more workers in uniform out on the streets. As well as policemen and postmen, there would be lots of firefighters and ambulance workers out to deal with emergencies. There were also some new kinds of uniform, like that of the ARP (Air Raid

Precautions) wardens whose job was to make sure that people stuck to the rules about the black-out and air raids. Other people became 'fire watchers', an important job when so many fire bombs were falling: a fire watcher kept lookout for small fires and was trained to put them out before they spread. Army bomb disposal squads also appeared in the streets, to deal with bombs which had dropped without exploding. And to help keep all these emergency workers going, volunteers ran tea vans and mobile canteens, handing out precious hot cuppas and food.

The Women's Voluntary Service run a free canteen for people during the Blitz.

What else did people do to stay safe during the Blitz?

If you were walking around a city during the Blitz, you might notice other oddities, even in the daytime. Windows might have crosses made of masking tape on them, to help stop them shattering dangerously in a bomb blast. You could also keep an eye out for signs to the nearest public air-raid shelter, so you would know where to go if you heard the warning that a raid was about to begin.

Many air-raid shelters in London had blue lights so they were easy to spot at night.

How many people can you fit in an air-raid shelter?

That all depends on what sort of shelter it is.

When bombers were sighted on their way to attack a city, air-raid sirens would make a loud wailing sound to warn people to get to safety. Many of the public air-raid shelters had brick walls and strong concrete roofs. Many people felt safest underground; coal cellars, Underground stations and even the crypts underneath churches were all used as public shelters. In Kent, thousands of people used ancient caves as air-raid shelters, with special trains laid on to take Londoners out to their new cosy night-time home from home.

If that all sounds like too much fuss, people could also have their own air-raid shelters at home. There were two types, named after two government ministers, the Anderson and the Morrison (although the Morrison was not in use until towards the end of the Blitz).

People sheltering from an air raid on the platforms of the London Underground.

Inside an Anderson shelter:

- Walls: two curved pieces of corrugated metal, fixed together at the top, and half buried under ground.
- 45cm of earth covering the walls.

- Strong barrier in front of the door adds extra protection.

Good points: handy; safe from most things except a direct hit by a bomb; blended into the garden (keen gardeners could grow vegetables in the earth on top of the shelter).

Bad points: not much room; often damp and flooded; didn't protect you from the deafening noise of an air raid, no good for people without a garden.

Inside a Morrison shelter:

- Handy size for use inside the home — can double up as a table.
- Strong steel on top and wire mesh on sides.

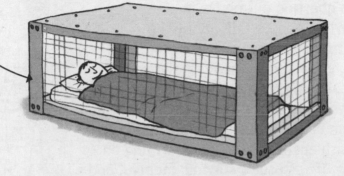

Good points: shelterers didn't have to leave the house in bad weather; easy to assemble.

Bad points: not very roomy, the Morrison shelter only slept two adults and one child.

Take a look at a very important part of this Morrison shelter: the mattress and pillow inside!

Even for people who were lucky not to have their houses bombed, the Blitz meant months of disturbed nights and extreme tiredness. One survey, from September 1940, found that two out of every three people in London were getting less than four hours' sleep a night.

Usually, constant danger and no sleep makes people exhausted instead of brave and jolly. So you might be surprised to hear about the 'Blitz Spirit' . . .

What was the Blitz Spirit?

This is one of those things that most grown-ups think they know about — if you have one handy, go and try this question out on them.

When people talk about the Blitz Spirit, they usually mean the bravery and good humour shown by those living through the Blitz. Night after night, the story goes, Hitler's air force bombed British cities, and the British answered back by carrying on with life as usual, staying cheerful and even making jokes about the bombs and the black-out.

This isn't the whole story. It's true that there were plenty of jokes swapped in the air-raid shelters, and some shelters were known to be the place to go for a sing-song and a party atmosphere. And many people did

An air-raid warden and Rip the dog demonstrate how to look for victims trapped in bombed-out houses following an air raid.

try to look after each other and to carry on with their lives in spite of everything. But there were also plenty of people who left the cities to go somewhere safer — tens of thousands of people from East London ended up in Oxford during the Blitz. And not everyone was looking after their neighbours. Dark nights and damaged buildings were so tempting for burglars that the crime rates actually rose during the war.

How many elephants could you fit in an air-raid shelter?

The answer is, not many — so London Zoo sent as many of its animals as it could away to safety before the bombing started. Lots were sent to Whipsnade Zoo in Bedfordshire.

What other places or organizations needed protection from air raids?

All sorts of things had to be kept safe from the air raids. Important institutions like the BBC and the Bank of England moved their headquarters out to the countryside at the start of the war. And the National Gallery moved its most precious paintings to a Welsh slate quarry.

What did people eat in wartime?

Not the same things as you do now, I expect!

Before the war, people in Britain ate lots of things which you probably eat today, like roast dinners, fish and chips, and sandwiches. But today we eat all sorts of different food as well, mostly from other countries, which people in 1930s Britain would have been confused by. There wasn't much pasta, hummus or chicken tikka masala on offer.

Even ordinary food became harder to find once the war started. In 1940, the government introduced food rationing, so that soon you could only get a small amount each week of meat, sugar, tea and butter. More types of food got added to the list as the war went on, and fruit like oranges and bananas disappeared from the shops.

Tray containing a ration book and the weekly ration of sugar, tea, margarine, 'national butter', lard, eggs, bacon and cheese as issued to an adult in Britain during 1942.

Why wasn't there enough food?

Blame globalization. By 1939, Britain had got used to bringing in almost 70 per cent of its food from abroad by ship. But as the war went on, it got more and more difficult for this food to get to Britain. Ships that used to travel around Europe and through the Mediterranean could no longer make the journey once Hitler was in charge of most of Europe.

What about basic stuff, like onions? There must have been enough of those to go round?

Even onions became a luxury, because the onion sellers who used to arrive in Britain each year could no longer come once Germany had invaded France, and British farmers didn't have the right seeds to grow their own.

The other serious problem with bringing food in by ship was that all ships heading for Britain were in danger of being attacked by German submarines or aeroplanes. On the very first day of the war, the first British ship was hit by a torpedo from a German submarine. As time went on, this danger got worse; by summer 1940, the fight between British ships and German submarines was so intense that it was called 'the Battle of the Atlantic'. Sailors have always faced risks when they go to sea, but during the war, working on a ship transporting food meant deadly peril on every voyage. Only essential journeys were worth the risk.

With less food coming in from abroad, British farmers had to work extremely hard to feed everyone at home using the same amount of farm land. This meant they could raise fewer animals for meat, because feeding animals uses more land than growing plant food for humans. For most of the country, steak was off the menu.

Phew!

So what could you eat instead?

Well, you could always eat your greens!

All the things that could be grown in Britain were suddenly top of the list of tasty treats, and vegetables weren't rationed. Posters like this one encouraged everyone to 'grow your own' in gardens and allotments. Growing veg was an important way to help keep yourself strong and healthy for the 'war effort', which explains the slogan 'Dig for Victory' — in wartime, even gardeners could be heroes. Allotments were a huge success. All sorts of public places were dug up to make space for growing veg, even the moat of the Tower of London.

The government even decided to invent fun cartoon characters to get people eating more vegetables. 'Potato Pete' and 'Dr Carrot' appeared on posters and on the radio, telling the world

I make a good Soup!

Says 'POTATO PETE'

how great they were at making delicious meals and building healthy bodies.

One problem was that in spite of all these great adverts for lovely healthy potatoes, lots of people still loved eating meat. You probably have friends who are vegetarian; maybe you don't eat meat yourself. But in the 1940s, vegetarianism was much less popular. When the usual cuts of meat got harder to buy in wartime, hungry shoppers and diners had to be inventive. People with gardens could 'grow their own' by keeping rabbits or chickens; chickens were especially useful as they could provide regular eggs as well as a precious roast dinner. Anyone who didn't have a garden could still get in on the trend by joining a Pig Club, where a group of people kept a pig together, feeding it on scraps and then getting a share of the resulting bacon and sausages.

Eating your pets! Yuck! What other meat did people eat?

If you don't like the idea of eating a rabbit you'd kept in your garden, you probably wouldn't fancy some of the other kinds of meat which ended up on wartime dinner tables. SPAM was a new tinned food  from America, which got its name from a shortening of **sp**iced **ham**. Another new mystery tinned food, called 'snoek', appeared in British shops shortly after the war. A type of fish from South Africa, it was unappetizingly smelly and not very popular. Horse meat cropped up on restaurant menus, and one cinema chain in London put 'Roast Eagle and Veg' on the menu when they got an interesting new meat from their supplier.

Could you still buy sweets?

A particularly important question for wartime kids, who were just as keen on sugary goodies

as children today. In 1942, a dark day came for the children of Britain when sweet rationing was introduced. Everyone could have 50g of sweets or chocolate each *week* — that's about half a Twix. Some generous grown-ups who didn't like sweets might give their rations to children. American soldiers posted to Britain were often a handy source of treats, as they were issued plenty of sweets. And some people made them at home, stretching out the sugar rations by using honey or condensed milk instead.

An American soldier shares sweets with some British children.

Were any *good* new sweets invented using rationed ingredients?

It depends what you mean by 'good'! Carrot brittle and carrot jam both appeared when there were plenty of carrots to go around but not enough sugar!

Carrot jam wasn't the only weird substitute food around. Coffee-starved citizens in Europe and Germany made out of ground-up acorns instead of coffee beans. And when tea got too scarce in wartime Jersey, those who were truly desperate for a cuppa tried making it out of dried blackberry leaves.

Where was the 'Black Market'?

Almost everywhere — and it could be hard to spot. A 'black market' means any illegal trading of goods which the law controls. So if the law says you're not allowed to sell alcohol, for instance, without paying a tax to the government, then shopkeepers who sell it but don't pay tax are selling 'on the black market'. During the war, when so many different things were rationed, there was a bustling black market. If you didn't have enough coupons in your ration book, but knew the right butcher and had enough money, you could get hold of that juicy steak that your neighbours couldn't. If you had the cash and didn't mind risking a guilty conscience, you could still buy the things you needed or wanted, and many people did!

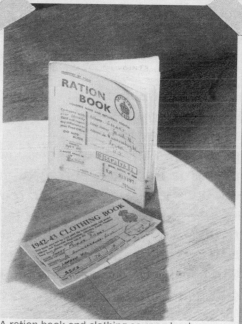

A ration book and clothing coupon book.

What was the 'National Loaf' – and was there enough for everyone?

Plenty of things were sold to the public as being healthy superfoods during the war, but that wasn't always the full story. The 'National Loaf' was the name the government gave to a particular type of wholemeal bread, which they said was much more nutritious than white bread. The problem was, people hated it. They complained that it was too dark and gave them indigestion.

Wholemeal bread is indeed better for you than white bread, but that wasn't the main reason the government were so keen for everyone to eat it: to make white flour, you have to take out part of the wheat grain — so you get less flour from the same amount of wheat. So, dark healthy National Loaves wasted less food than the fluffy white sort people preferred in their sandwiches.

Was everyone skinny during the war?

Winston Churchill was never slim – even during the war.

Not everyone. Winston Churchill, who became Prime Minister in 1940, managed to keep his famously round shape all through the war! On average, people were thinner in the 1940s than they are now, but that doesn't mean that everyone was wasting away on rations. In fact, there's evidence that the wartime diet was better for you than either the food we eat now, or even the food people were eating before the war. During the war, British people drank more milk, ate more vegetables, and ate less meat and sugar. And for poorer people, who hadn't eaten so well before the war, rationing meant they could get fairer shares.

A typical meal during the Second World War.

A typical meal today.

However much people in Britain complained about their boring food and chewy bread, they were still lucky compared to lots of other countries. In Holland, by 1944/45 people were so hungry that they ate tulip bulbs. And in France, there had been so little good food around in wartime that by 1944 the average height of kids had got shorter, by eleven centimetres for girls and seven centimetres for boys.

Was it hard to buy other things, apart from food?

Yes! It got difficult to buy most things after a while. From toys and babies' bottles to blankets and bedsheets, from petrol to soap, everything was hard to get. Even paper was scarce; newspapers were only four pages long by the end of the war, and even when schools were open, there weren't enough textbooks to go around.

Like food, clothes were rationed — most people could only buy a few new clothes, and had to make do with the ones they had, even when they were old and worn out. The US government published a booklet to prepare American soldiers to go to England in 1942, and told them: 'If British civilians look dowdy and badly dressed, it is not because they do not like good clothes or know how to wear them. All clothing is rationed . . . Old clothes are "good form".' To save on cloth, any clothes that could be bought new had to be smaller than they used to be — skirts were narrower, jackets were shorter, pockets were reduced, and men weren't even allowed to have stylish turn-ups on their trousers. Dapper men were so annoyed about this that questions were asked in Parliament about whether it was really necessary.

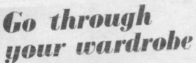

What was Shanks' Pony?

This poster explains it.

Still confused? It helps if you know that 'shanks' is an old word for 'legs'. So 'Shanks' Pony' was a jokey way of saying that instead of riding somewhere on a pony, you were using your legs to get around.

There were good reasons why the government was advertising walking — they weren't just trying to get people fit. Firstly, hardly anyone had cars, and those who did usually couldn't get the petrol to make them go. Right from the start of the war,

petrol was rationed. Like food, it had to be brought in from abroad, so there was less of it to go around. Any petrol was needed for important war work, like moving soldiers and vital equipment around. So most people who owned a car put it away in the garage for the war, as they wouldn't be using it anyway.

Of course, you could always get the train or the bus. But there weren't too many of those around either, because trains and buses also need fuel, and they were also being used to move soldiers and war workers around the country. Posters went up, nagging passengers to ask 'Is Your Journey Really Necessary?' in the hope they would decide to stay at home instead and stop clogging up the packed trains. Or, like the 'Shanks' Pony' poster says, to walk if they only had a short distance to go.

If your journey is REALLY necessary and you can choose your times travel between

10 & 4

What about riding a bike?

Well, if you couldn't get where you were going by car, train or bus, you might decide to get on your bike and use pedal power to get there. But — you guessed it — it's not that easy. If you needed to buy a new bike you might be stuck. With less metal free for use in non-war factories, and factory workers going off to war, the number of bikes on sale dropped just when they would have been really handy.

So, if you wanted to make sure you got where you wanted to go in wartime, it had to be by Shanks' Pony.

What was the war like for children?

It was exciting, and scary, and so different from life now it's hard to imagine.

You've probably heard of evacuation, when hundreds of thousands of children were sent away from the cities to the countryside so that they would be safe from German bombs. This was the biggest change in life for a huge number of everyday kids — on just one day, Friday 1 September 1939, 1.5 million people were packed up into trains and buses and taken miles from home. Whole schools went all together, and while some children had their mothers with them if they were babies or had baby brothers and sisters, most of the evacuees had to say goodbye to their mums and dads without knowing when they would see them again.

Evacuees from Bristol to Kingsbridge, Devon, 1940.

Why did evacuees have to wear labels?

Before they left, all evacuees had to be given a label with their name and address on it. So many children were going to be shifted around the country without very many adults to keep track of them that labels were needed to stop them getting lost or muddled up. And the good news is, it seems to have worked: newspapers from the time report that only one evacuee was accidentally mislaid! Luckily, the poor child was eventually found again.

When they got to the countryside, the evacuees were mostly tired, hungry and dirty, and things didn't necessarily get better. Everything had been organized in such a hurry that there wasn't a plan for where each child should stay; a coachload of evacuees might be taken to a village hall to stand around waiting while the local people chose the children who looked the most obedient, or neatest, or strongest if they wanted a helper for their farm. Anyone who's ever been picked last for a sports team will be able to imagine how that might feel.

For some children, evacuation was a miserable experience: miles away from all their family and friends, many evacuees ended up staying in cold, dirty houses, or with unfriendly adults who treated them like servants, or just feeling horribly homesick. Others had a fantastic time. Many city kids loved being able to run around in the countryside, and there was often more fresh food to be had in the country. If they were lucky enough to stay with friendly hosts, evacuation could be a bit like a good holiday.

Some evacuees learned about farming.

Were all children evacuated?

Not all children were evacuated, and for those who stayed in the cities, life could be even more like a holiday. There weren't enough teachers around, because so many male teachers had gone away to fight in the war. So school was often cancelled, or run with shorter hours. Sometimes, schools were evacuated to the countryside, so pupils who were left behind didn't get many lessons. In the cities, school buildings were sometimes turned into rescue centres or stations for the emergency services. Even though you only had to be 14 to finish school, many wartime kids didn't even manage to stay at school for that long.

What did wartime kids do for fun?

A long holiday from school might
sound like fun — but remember,
this is before games consoles were
invented, so children had to make
do with a book, a jigsaw or an exciting game of
snakes and ladders. It was often more fun to make
your own entertainment out of the house. Hanging
around in the streets could be far from boring when
there was a war on. British
and German aeroplanes
zoomed low overhead,
and kids learned to tell
the differences between them — British planes had
a circle on the wings, where German planes had
a cross and a swastika on the tail. Spotting the
different types of plane was a popular hobby. Kids
living in the south-east of England during the Battle
of Britain could even watch whole battles from
their windows, as British and German pilots fought
in the skies.

That sounds scary! What else did wartime kids get up to?

After an air raid, many town and city children ran out to hunt for shrapnel — pieces of the shells fired by anti-aircraft guns. This was a dangerous hobby, as shrapnel was very sharp and could burn you if it was 'fresh'. But for some kids, risk only made wartime more exciting. Gangs of young people left behind when everyone else was evacuated were known as 'Dead

Posters warned people not to talk about the war to anyone – just in case they were a spy!

End Kids' (after a popular American film from the 1930s), and they found all sorts of hair-raising new pastimes. In Wapping, East London, one gang of Dead End Kids got together to form a volunteer fire brigade and ran around putting out firebombs during air raids. Which is definitely not something to try at home.

What did spies do in the war?

Spying isn't all drinking cocktails and wearing fancy clothes, whatever you might think if you've seen a James Bond film. In wartime, spies (and the whole of the intelligence services) have an especially vital part to play. If you're trying to win a war, you have to be clever about it; it's not enough just to have more soldiers or better guns than your enemy, if their tactics are always one step ahead of yours.

The intelligence services in the Second World War had three main jobs:
1. to find out what the enemy was up to;
2. to make sure the enemy couldn't find out what you were up to;
3. to convince the enemy you were up to something totally different — this is called 'spreading misinformation'.

Spies could be anyone – from famous actresses and actors to ordinary people next door.

107

So how did spies find out what the enemy was doing?

Mostly this comes under the heading of 'listening in' to work out what the other side is planning to do next. If you overhear a message saying there's a big attack coming, for example, you can get ready by making sure your troops are in the right place beforehand. But you can also simply watch to see where the enemy's going.

The British used several different methods to check up on their enemies. When the German air force was attacking in the Battle of Britain, early warnings were vital. They meant that British pilots would have time to 'scramble' — jump into their planes and fly to where the Germans were, to tackle them before they could attack. One of the simplest methods was stationing people around the coast with binoculars, watching for planes over the Channel. The most high-tech method, and the most secretive, was radar. RADAR stood for **RA**dio **D**etection **A**nd **R**anging, and it wasn't listening in on radio signals sent by the other side — instead, radar stations used radio waves to find out where physical objects like planes and submarines were. Each station had a transmitter and a receiver: the transmitter sent out a radio signal, which kept going until it reached a solid object and then bounced back towards the radar station and its receiver. By checking how long it took for the signal to get to the object and back again, staff at the station could work out how far it had travelled.

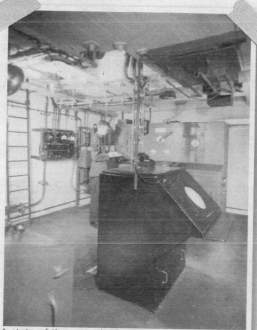

A state-of-the-art radar installation. The monitor is the big wooden box in the middle of the room.

So if a radar station sent a signal out into the air, and it bounced back, it could well have found

a plane. As more signals were sent and received, the intelligence services could tell how many planes there were in the group, and which direction they were headed in.

Who invented radar technology?

Radio technology had been around since the start of the twentieth century, but using it to find objects with radar was totally new. Radar was invented in the 1930s by British scientists, so that by the time the war started there was already a line of radar stations along the south and east coasts of England. Another invention in 1940 meant that better, smaller radar kits were possible, so that as the war went on, ships and aeroplanes could have their own portable radar systems.

Having radar technology was a huge advantage for Britain. In the Battle of Britain, instead of having to keep aeroplanes in the sky over the coast at all times to watch out for German planes, the British could wait for a warning to come in from

These air force pilots are 'scrambling' to get planes off the ground as soon as possible.

the radar stations and then 'scramble' aircraft from an RAF base. The British government tried very hard not to let on about their fantastic new invention and all the clever things they were able to do with it, so that they could stay one step ahead. Radar wasn't officially public knowledge in Britain until 1945, and while the Germans could see that there were some sort of radio towers all along the coast, they didn't know exactly what they did.

The 360ft transmitter towers at Bawdsey Chain home radar station, 1945.

111

How else did the British try and hide the invention of radar?

Once radar became small enough to be installed in aeroplanes, the British came up with a simple explanation for how their pilots were able to 'see' German planes at night: they ate a lot of carrots! Apparently, carrots were so good for night vision because of all the Vitamin A they contain.

So many people believed this rumour that you might even have been told it yourself — but rest assured, it's not true, it's just more of that 'misinformation'. Fighter pilots also helped to keep the myth alive by taking Vitamin A tablets, and wearing special protective glasses, whenever journalists were around.

Each side was very keen to listen in on the other side's communication systems. If you sent a letter in wartime, you couldn't expect it to be private. Any letters could be opened and read; huge numbers of people were employed to check letters in case a German spy was disguising his reports as postcards to his auntie.

Radio systems weren't too hard to tap into, either. But once a spy had got hold of a message, that was only the beginning of the job: any important messages would be in code.

How did spies crack secret codes?

This was an enormously important question which each country was asking itself at the start of the war. Secrecy was so important that inventing clever new codes, and cracking those used by the enemy, could make enough difference to win or lose the war.

What was the Enigma code?

The Germans started the war with
a particularly brilliant set of codes.
They worked a bit like codes you've
probably come across before, where
you swap each letter of the alphabet
for a different one. So, you might
decide to write 'F' instead of 'A', for
example. You need to make sure the
person you're writing to knows which letters to
swap for the right ones, by giving them a list of the
swapped letters, called a 'key'. Then you can send
messages to each other which are hard for other
people to read.

The problem with that kind of code is that it's
pretty easy to crack. Anyone who finds the message
can have a guess at what
some of the words might
be, and if they guess one
or two of the letters right,
they can find out what
all the other letters are.
Over the years, military
bosses had paid
maths whizzes
to invent
all sorts
of more
complicated

114

codes to combat this problem.

The special, super-secret codes which the Germans used involved using an ingenious machine called Enigma. The name shows how tough the code was — an 'enigma' is a puzzle or a mystery. Enigma didn't just swap the letters in a message around once; instead, it used several different wheels with letters of the alphabet around the edges to scramble it several times. Each time an Enigma operator typed in a letter, it was processed by all the wheels.

A Second World War German 'Enigma' cipher machine.

So, if 'F' meant 'A' in one part of the message, that didn't help you work out what 'F' meant everywhere else. The result was a code that was maddeningly difficult to untangle. To add to the security, the Germans used different keys for the Enigma machines and changed the keys regularly, so that they could be using a new code before anyone had had a chance to crack the last one.

How did the British crack the Enigma code?

Luckily, the British also had a secret weapon: a large number of highly intelligent men and women. Based at Bletchley Park near Milton Keynes, the top-secret codebreaking teams included maths students, language experts and people who were extremely good at solving crosswords. They also had a head-start from codebreakers from Poland who had

Bletchley Park.

managed to crack the secrets of an old version of the Enigma machine. And it became clear that there was one important chink in the armour of the German codes: the Enigma machine could never encode a letter as the same letter it started from. An 'A' could go through the machine and come out as an 'F', an 'X' or an 'E', but never as an 'A'. It doesn't sound like much, but it was a clue.

Even for a team like this, cracking an Enigma code still needed lots and lots and lots of maths, which took a very long time to do when most calculations were done with a pencil and a piece of paper.

How did the codebreakers speed up their sums?

To crunch the numbers more quickly, the team at Bletchley Park designed a machine called the 'Bombe' which could run through possible combinations of letters much faster than a team of humans could. When the Germans came up with a new and better code machine, called the 'Lorenz', the Bletchley boffins invented a machine called 'Colossus' — an early version of a computer. It's hard to imagine our world without computers now — and that's just one of the reasons to be grateful to the codebreakers.

Once the British could decode messages from Enigma machines, they could listen in on the Germans' top-secret messages. They could find out where German submarines were, so that British ships could avoid them. Decoded messages from Bletchley Park even told the British when and where any German spies were planning to arrive in Britain, so that they could send a welcoming party to catch them!

This work was so secret that the people who worked at Bletchley Park weren't allowed to tell anyone what they'd been doing for over thirty years afterwards. But they could be very proud of what they did: Winston Churchill thought the decoded messages were so precious, he called them his 'golden eggs'. Some historians think the war might have gone on for at least two years longer if it hadn't been for the brainboxes of Bletchley Park.

How else could you stop the enemy listening in?

The easiest way, of course, is not to say anything in the first place! With so many spies trying to work out what their enemies were up to, and so many service-men and women moving around the world in the war, any gossip about where people were going or what they were doing could get back to the enemy. And if, for instance, the Germans found out

"**Keep it under your hat!**"

CARELESS TALK COSTS LIVES

that a factory in Britain was being used to make an important new weapon, it could become a target for bombers. So the simplest way to stop the enemy finding out secret information was to stop people at home from talking about it.

The most famous campaign started by the British government used posters to spread the word that 'Careless Talk Costs Lives'. In America, the government used the catchy slogan 'Loose

Lips Sink Ships' to warn people not to gossip about where sailors were heading. These phrases were so catchy, in fact, that you might still hear people using them today.

What's a double agent?

Double agents are spies who are fooling the people who think they're the spy's bosses. Confused? That's sort of the idea.

For instance, one daring double agent of the Second World War was Eddie Chapman, code-named 'Agent Zigzag', who convinced the Germans that he wanted to work for them. He trained as a German spy and was trusted on highly secret missions; the Germans even awarded him a medal, the Iron Cross. They didn't suspect the truth: Eddie Chapman was really working for the British.

He's on our side.

Adolf Hitler.

Eddie Chapman, code-named 'Agent Zigzag'.

He's on our side.

Winston Churchill.

What kinds of things did double agent Eddie Chapman do?

He passed German secrets back to London, and helped the British government by spreading misinformation. When the Germans fired V-1 flying bombs at London, Chapman helped to convince them that the missiles were landing too far north and missing the city. The Germans adjusted their aim, and the bombs started falling to the south of central London instead.

Some misinformation campaigns were so bold, they sound totally ridiculous. Operation Mincemeat was a bizarre plan to dress up the dead body of a homeless man as a British officer, handcuff him to a briefcase stuffed with maps and plans saying that the British were going to invade Greece (instead of Sicily, which was the real plan), and then leave the body floating in the sea near Spain for the Germans to find. Even more bizarrely, it worked. The invasion of Sicily took the Germans by surprise and went much better for the Allies than it could have done without a handy dead body.

In 1944, the Allies put

together a plan for a huge invasion of Europe, starting with France, which by then had been occupied by the Germans for four years. On 'D-Day', 6 June 1944, tens of thousands of Allied troops would land on the beaches of Normandy or be dropped there from aeroplanes. The last thing they wanted was for the Germans to be lying in wait for them, but the Germans knew that something was up and an invasion was about to begin. So the Allies used double agents to make Hitler think that they were going to land in a different part of France.

The Allied invasion of Normandy, D-Day, 6 June 1944.

And thanks to the codebreakers at Bletchley Park, the Allied commanders could listen in on the Germans' communications and check that they had swallowed the misinformation story. Luckily for the Allied soldiers, the Germans fell for it, and the Normandy landings were the beginning of the end of the war in Europe.

Who were the Magic Gang?

Jasper Maskelyne, conjuror, illusionist and master of disguise, was an unlikely recruit to the British intelligence forces. He wore a top hat and carried a magic wand, which isn't the typical stuff a spy wears to blend in. At first, he did put on magic shows for the troops, but soon he turned his magical talents into a top-secret weapon for the Allies.

Maskelyne and his assistants (known as 'The Magic Gang') were sent to join the British army in the Egyptian Desert, where they set to work making fake aeroplanes and tanks to confuse the enemy.

Some of the gang had experience of building sets in theatres, and with their help Maskelyne constructed amazing scenery to befuddle the enemy.

Jasper Maskelyne's greatest triumph came in 1942, when he helped the Allies to win the Battle of El Alamein. The British were planning to attack the Germans from the north, so Jasper's job was to convince them that there was a huge British army waiting to strike from the south instead. As well as thousands of fake tanks, the Magic Gang built a very convincing water pipeline heading towards the pretend army, to take water to the soldiers. But cleverly, they stopped the pipeline halfway. When the German planes flew over and saw this, they decided there was no way the pipeline would be ready for a few weeks — so the German commander, Rommel, took some time off as sick leave. As soon as he was out of the way, the British attacked with their real army, in the north, and won the battle.

Who won the war?

The Allies. I bet you knew this one
really, though. If the Allies hadn't
won, life today would be
very different indeed.

There are all sorts of
reasons why the Allies won.
Was it all because Germany tried
to bite off more than it could
chew, and fight too many battles
at once? Was it because the USA
joined the Allies, with all that
American money and factory power
to provide weapons? Was it all down
to the Russians? Or to the Allies'
air forces, bombing Germany's
factories? Or even to the Allied
codebreakers' enormous brains? Historians can
argue endlessly about which reasons were most
important, and there isn't just one answer.

The end of the war came in 1945. To win,
the Allies had to beat both Germany and Japan.
Germany was the first to fall. In April 1945, Soviet
troops surrounded Berlin, trapping Hitler. He killed
himself before the Allies could reach him, and
Germany surrendered to the Allies on 7 May 1945.

The next day was officially called Victory in
Europe Day, or VE Day for short. Huge parties
started straight away. Winston Churchill gave

Britain the good news over the radio, and crowds headed into the cities to celebrate. In London, thousands of people flocked to Buckingham Palace to see the king and queen; Trafalgar Square filled up with overjoyed dancers; and bomber aeroplanes swooped over the city in a victory flight.

Winston Churchill waves to the crowds on VE Day.

How did other Allied countries celebrate?

All over the Allied countries, the streets were full of banners, bunting and dancing, and many people went to church to give thanks for the peace.

But the war against Japan in Asia still wasn't finished. Three months after the surrender of the Germans, the Americans used a new weapon that would kill thousands of Japanese civilians in one go: the atomic bomb (see page 68). On 6 August an American bomber dropped an atomic bomb over the Japanese city of Hiroshima, and another bomb was dropped on Nagasaki three days later. Japan officially surrendered on 14 August, and 15 August 1945 became Victory in Japan (or 'VJ') Day. The Second World War was *finally* over.

When did the Allies know they were winning?

For the first couple of years of the war, the prospect didn't look good for the Allies. The Germans seemed to have better technology and were sweeping through Europe at a shocking pace. In the summer of 1940, Hitler defeated the French, and started sending his air force over to soften up the Brits so that he could invade them next. Suddenly, Britain didn't seem to have many allies at all, and the future was pretty cloudy.

129

So what changed?

In December 1941, two things happened which made a very big difference. First, the Soviets began to turn the tide against the Germans who had invaded Russia in the summer. The Germans had taken the Russian leader, Stalin, by surprise when they sent three million men on the attack — this was a huge shock given that up until then, Stalin thought he and Hitler were on the same side. Now, the Russians were on the side of the Allies. By the start of December the Germans had got almost as far as Moscow — but then, on 6 December, the Russians sent in a whole army they had been keeping hidden, and beat the

Stalin was the Russian dictator.

Germans in a dramatic battle. Just one day later, the Japanese bombed an important American naval base on Hawaii, called Pearl Harbor. The American Pacific Fleet of ships and sailors was devastated by the attack, which killed 2,403 servicemen. Now that the USA was under attack, it had to join in the war. British Prime Minister Winston Churchill met with American President Franklin D. Roosevelt in December 1941, and the Allies now had another huge, rich country on their side.

By 1943 the leaders of the three main Allied powers (that's America, Britain and Russia) were so hopeful about the situation that they had a meeting to decide what to do once they'd won the war. From this point on, they were convinced that they would win — it was just a question of how long it would take. As the months went on, the Allies won several vitally important battles.

What battles did the Allies win that made winning the war possible?

In 1942, the American navy defeated the Japanese in the Pacific Ocean at the Battle of Midway in June; in early November, the British beat the Germans in the desert, at El Alamein in Egypt; and in September, the battle between the Russians and the Germans to take control of the city of Stalingrad began. After a long, freezing winter of fighting, the Germans surrendered in February 1943. It was a shocking loss for the Germans, and

The Bény-sur-Mer Canadian War Cemetery. The cemetery contains predominantly Canadian soldiers killed during the D-Day landings.

now it looked almost certain that they would lose the war.

Still, as the obvious but true saying goes, it's not over till it's over. Both Germany and Japan were able to keep on fighting for a long time, and they really, really didn't want to give up. As the Allies liberated Western Europe and fought their way right into Germany, as the Soviets advanced through Eastern Europe, and as the Americans bombed Japan, the Allies were fairly certain they would win the war — but no one wanted to celebrate until it was definitely, finally over and the killing had stopped. And even when VE Day and VJ Day did come, after all that pain and loss, many people didn't feel like celebrating anyway.

What did the winners do to the losers?

When at long last the Allies finally won the war, after six years of horrible fighting, whole cities destroyed by bombs, huge loss of life, and a massively expensive war effort, they had to decide what to do next. They could have chosen to punish the Axis powers, Germany and Japan, for all the destruction, and for starting the war in the first place. And they also had the chance to decide who would be in charge of the losing countries now.

At first, the Allies took over the government of both Japan and Germany. Britain, America, France and Russia couldn't agree on who should run Germany, so a few years after the war they decided to split the whole country down the middle. West Germany was run by America, Britain and France, and East Germany was run by the Soviet Russians. Even the capital city, Berlin, was split in two, so that East Berlin and West Berlin were two separate cities. In just a few years, Communist Russia became the Western powers' new Number One enemy, and America's

The building of the Berlin Wall.

biggest fear was that more of the world would turn Communist. The division between the Communist and capitalist countries was so enormous that in 1961 the East German government built a huge wall all the way through the city, with guards keeping lookout so that no one could cross from the east to the west without permission — although thousands of people tried. Many people couldn't visit their families on the other side of the wall for years. The Berlin Wall stayed standing until 1989, the year before East and West Germany became one country again.

The Berlin Wall in the 1990s.

135

So were the Germans and Japanese punished after all?

Right after the war, the Allies did want to punish some of the Germans and Japanese who were responsible for the worst acts of the Second World War. They held war crimes trials, so that high-up Nazis and the men who were in charge of death camps or inhumane camps for prisoners of war had to go to court and be sentenced to go to prison, or even to death. Both Germany and Japan were stripped of any overseas or annexed territories (land) and were not allowed to have *any* armed forces at all, while smaller Axis countries were only permitted to keep very small armed forces. But the more difficult question was: How do you punish a whole country? And *should* you?

The Allies had good reasons not to get carried away with getting revenge on their enemies. After all, if they made the Axis give up everything they had, they could have become extremely poor countries filled with very angry people — a recipe for more war, which no one wanted. Plus, America and Britain really didn't want the German and Japanese people to hate them, in case they decided to become Communists and take sides with the other big Communist countries, Russia or (after 1949) China.

So what did the Allies do instead?

Instead of punishing all the German and Japanese people for the war, the Americans and British decided it would be best to help them. As soon as the war ended, the Americans started giving lots of money to the countries they had only just stopped fighting. This may seem strange, but it was actually very sensible. If the Americans helped the losing countries to get back on their feet, so they could build factories and start making money again, then they would be more likely to be friends with America and to trade with them. That meant more money and less trouble for the US in the long run. This move wasn't just kind; more importantly, it worked. Both Germany and Japan made lots of money in the second half of the twentieth century, and were two of the world's great economic success stories.

Britain, on the other hand, had put so much money and effort into fighting the war that it ended up too poor to stay as the powerful world leader it had been before the war. Soon, there wasn't much left of the British Empire. Just because you win a war, doesn't mean you get to have everything your own way.

How did the war change Great Britain?

Britain was changed forever by the Second World War. If you keep your eyes open, you can find evidence of the war all over the place. Some of the changes were huge: the National Health Service was set up after the war, and before that you had to pay whenever you needed to see a doctor. Any time you get medicine for free, you can chalk it up as a result of the Second World War.

If you've got more questions about the war, there are lots of museums to visit — you could have a whole year's worth of fun war-themed day-trips if you fancied travelling all over the country. Of course, you should start with the Imperial War Museum in London, or the IWM North in Manchester, where you can find out all about the war, both about the fighting and about everyday life. If you're a fan of aeroplanes, there's the IWM in Duxford, Cambridgeshire; you can go aboard a Second World War navy ship at HMS *Belfast* on the Thames in London; and at the Churchill War Rooms in London you can nose around the underground rooms where the British government worked from during the Blitz.

There are all sorts of other places to visit around the country, like Bletchley Park in Buckinghamshire where codebreakers worked in secret, and Eden Camp in Yorkshire where Italian and German prisoners were held.

HMS *Belfast* is now a museum on the Thames in London.

What can you still see from the Second World War today?

You can seek out traces of the war in your local area. Big cities often have special war memorials, sometimes just to remind people about the sacrifices made in the Second World War but more often including other wars, especially the First World War. In London, Belfast, Edinburgh and Cardiff, there are national memorials to visit for everyone who died in the war. If you're in London, you could look for some more particular memorials:

- The Women of World War II memorial in Whitehall is a sculpture of some of the uniforms worn by women in the war, hanging on pegs as if they've been taken off at the war's end.

Women in World War II Memorial, London.

- The National Firefighters' Memorial near St Paul's Cathedral was first built in honour of the firefighters who worked during the Blitz, but later became a memorial to all the firefighters who have died while on duty.

- The Animals' Memorial in Hyde Park was put up to say thank you to all the animals who played a part in the wars of the twentieth century, including some of the heroes on page 54.

There are also war memorials all over the country — most local churches will have a memorial nearby, or on a plaque inside the church. Places like large old railway stations and post offices also often have their own war memorial plaques, listing the names of the people who worked there who died in the war.

You might find evidence of pillboxes near where you live: these were concrete huts with small openings for windows, just big enough to look out of and fire a gun. Pillboxes were built near beaches and roads, to help defend Britain in case the Germans did invade. Sometimes they were used to guard a store of weapons or ammunition that was being kept for when the Allies invaded Europe.

What else might you find from the war?

If you find yourself flying
into England on a plane,
if you're low enough
over the South Coast or
East Anglia you might see
lots of small airfields with
runways. They're almost
certainly leftovers from the
Second World War, when RAF
aircraft coming back from
Europe could quickly run
out of fuel and so needed
somewhere close to the sea
to land.

Once you know what to
look for, you'll be able to
spot the traces of the Second
World War almost everywhere you go. If your town,
city or village has allotments where people can
grow vegetables, they may have been set up during
the war as part of the 'Dig for Victory' campaign.
Even if you're just walking down the street, keep
a lookout for tell-tale holes in the ground. A long,
thin concrete base with little holes in it at regular
intervals could be a sign that railings used to be
there, and were removed during the war to be
melted down for scrap metal.

If these are too hard to spot, try looking in your wardrobe for one of the smaller legacies of the war: if you own any T-shirts, it's thanks to the Second World War. Before the war, no one in Britain wore T-shirts — shirts had buttons down the front, and a proper collar. But when American soldiers were posted in Britain, they wore T-shirts underneath their uniforms. And the American soldiers, known as 'GIs', seemed incredibly cool to the poorer Brits in their shabby clothes. After the war, an off-duty GI wearing a T-shirt and sunglasses became the height of fashion, and trendy young people began to copy the look. From the big deals to the smallest trivia, after the Second World War, life would never be the same again.

How do I find out more?

The Imperial War Museum was set up in 1917 as a record of the First World War, and today it can give you a unique insight into what it was like to be involved in both the First and Second World Wars. If you can't make a trip to London to visit the Imperial War Museum, or to Manchester to visit IWM North, you could have a look at the museum's website.

The Imperial War Museum, London.

Other museums:

IWM Duxford, Cambridgeshire
The National Army Museum, London
The National Museum of the Royal Navy, Portsmouth
The Royal Air Force Museum, London, and Cosford,
    Shropshire
The Tank Museum, Bovington, Dorset

Websites:

www.iwm.org.uk
www.nationalarchives.gov.uk
www.cwgc.org

Books:

Tony Robinson's Weird World of Wonders:
    World War II by Tony Robinson
    (Macmillan, 2013)

Blitz — My Story: A Wartime Girl's Diary 1940–1941
    by Vince Cross
    (Scholastic, 2008)

Forgotten Voices of the Second World War
    by Max Arthur
    (Ebury Press, 2005)

Glossary

Adolf Hitler The leader of Germany during the Second World War

'Agent Zigzag' A British double agent who convinced the Germans he wanted to work for them

Air-raid shelter Reinforced shelters or designated underground areas to protect people during bombings

Air-raid sirens A siren to warn people that bombs might be dropped and to seek shelter

Allies The name used to refer to countries fighting alongside Britain during the war

Anderson shelter A type of air-raid shelter built in the garden and hidden under a layer of soil

ARP Air Raid Precaution wardens were in place to make sure people stuck to the rules about black-outs and air raids

Aryans Blond-haired and blue-eyed people. The Nazis believed that the Aryans were the most important 'race' of people

Atomic bomb A bomb which harnesses nuclear fusion — creating the most powerful weapon the world had ever seen

Axis The name given to the side fighting against the Allies. Germany, Japan and Italy were the main Axis powers

'Big Week' A campaign in 1944 where for six days the British and Americans sent thousands of aeroplanes to bomb German weapons factories

Black-out At night, all outside lights had to be turned off or covered up and all windows had to be covered with black blinds to stop light escaping — so that towns and cities could not be spotted from the air

Bletchley Park The building which housed the British codebreakers who eventually broke the Enigma code

Blitz The period of bombing between September 1940 and May 1941 when the German air force dropped over 100 tonnes of high explosives on British cities

Compassionate leave Extra time off given to soldiers with family problems

Conscription Where men of fighting age were made to join the war effort in one way or another

Dickin Medal An award given to animals for amazing service during the war

'Doodlebug' or V-1 Flying rockets containing explosives which were launched by the Germans

Enigma machine A machine used by the Germans to create complicated secret codes when sending messages

Evacuee A child sent away from a city to live in the countryside during the war

Franklin D. Roosevelt The US President during most of the Second World War

Gas masks Everyone in Britain was given a box with a gas mask in to protect them from poison gas

Geneva Convention An agreement signed by most countries following the First World War on the correct treatment of prisoners of war

Heinrich Himmler An important Nazi who was responsible for building and running the Nazi concentration camps

Hitler Youth The Nazi's youth organization

Holocaust An old word for sacrifice. During the Second World War, the Holocaust was the mass killing of up to six million Jewish people by the Nazis

Holy Grail A mythical cup with magical powers, which was supposed to have been missing for hundreds of years

Home Front Where ordinary people at home in Britain were involved in the war effort

Hurricane One of the types of fighter planes flown by the RAF

Imperial War Museum A museum set up in 1917 as a record of the First World War

Land Girls Women who worked on the land while the men were away fighting

'Little Boy' The first atomic bomb, which was dropped by the Americans on the Japanese city of Hiroshima, killing over 66,000 people

Luftwaffe The German air force — German for 'air weapon'

'Manhattan Project' A project set up by President Roosevelt to develop atomic weapons

Morrison shelter A type of air-raid shelter which could be built under a table inside the home

Nazis The German Fascist political party headed by Adolf Hitler

Neville Chamberlain The British Prime Minister at the start of the Second World War

Panzers Tanks designed by the German army

Pearl Harbor An important American base in Hawaii

that was bombed by the Japanese during the Second World War

POW Prisoner of war

POW camps The camps where the prisoners of war were kept

RADAR **RA**dio **D**etection **A**nd **R**anging used radio signals to find out where physical objects such as enemy planes and submarines were located

RAF The Royal Air Force of Britain

Rationing The system used to distribute fairly the limited amount of food, clothes and petrol available to people at home during the war

Red Cross food parcels These packages could be sent to prisoners of war and soldiers on the front lines and contained rations of food as well as toiletries

SPAM A type of tinned, spiced ham which was imported from America during the war

Spitfire A type of fighter plane flown by the RAF

VE Day Victory in Europe Day was declared on 8 May 1945, a day after Germany surrendered to the allies

Winston Churchill The British Prime Minister from 1940

Alphabetical index of main topics

Acknowledgements

With grateful thanks to Abigail Ratcliffe, Grant Rogers, Terry Charman and all those at IWM for their historical expertise, encouragement and support in making this book a reality.

Picture credits

Page 6 © IWM (HU 5234); 9 © IWM (EQU 4326); 11 Wikimedia Commons/USN; 15 © IWM (IA 37590); 21 © IWM (PST 14628); 23 Shutterstock/McCarthy's PhotoWorks; 24 © IWM (HU 006301); 25 © IWM (MH 13647); 26 © IWM (D 204); © IWM (CBM 1358); 28 © IWM (CH 1584); 30 (top) © IWM (CH 2621), (bottom) © IWM (MH 5190); 31 © IWM (CH 5291); 38 © IWM H 5694; 39 © IWM (E 6377); 44 © IWM (EPH 88); 46 Wikimedia Commons/Kevin Quinn; 48 (bottom) © IWM (PST 10025); 51 © IWM (H 14688); 53 © IWM (TR 193); 54 Rifleman Khan, reproduced by kind permission of Press Team (Scotland); 59 © IWM (BU 11451); 60 (top) © IWM (E 1715); 61 © IWM (STT 8025); 62 (top and bottom) Wikimedia Commons, (bottom) © IWM (TR 2161); 66 (top) Wikimedia Commons; 67 Wikimedia Commons; 68 (top) © IWM (MH 6809), (bottom) IWM (MH 29426); 70 © IWM (HU 18501.); 72 © IWM (PST 14622); 73 (top) © IWM (HU 1129), (bottom) © IWM (PST 13874); 74 © IWM (C 5422); 75 © IWM (D 21303); 76 (top) © IWM (PST 15290), reproduced by kind permission of The Royal Society for the Prevention of Accidents, www.rospa.com, (bottom) © IWM (PST 13850); 77 © IWM (D 2164); 78 © IWM (PST 13891); 79 © IWM (HU 672); 82 © IWM (D 5945); 85 © IWM (D 7958); 88 © IWM (PST 0696); 89 © IWM (PST 6080); © IWM (D 4921); 93 © IWM (D 11310); 94 © IWM (PST 20684); 95 © IWM (H 6550); 97 © IWM (PST 4773); 98 © IWM (PST 15265); 99 © IWM (PST 15293); 101 © IWM (D 2597); 103 © IWM (D 2473); 106 © IWM (PST 3363); 109 © IWM (CH 15189); 111 (top) © IWM (HU 104741), (bottom) © IWM (CH 15337); 115 © IWM (MH 27178); 116–117 Wikimedia Commons; 120 © IWM (PST 13953); 121 (left) © IWM (HU 5234), (middle) Wikimedia Commons, (right) Wikimedia Commons; 123 © IWM (A 24192); 127 © IWM (H 41849); 135 (top) © IWM (HU 73012).

Macmillan Children's Books is grateful for permission to reproduce copyright material. While every reasonable effort has been made to trace copyright holders, Macmillan would be pleased to hear from any not acknowledged.